In the Wake of the Day

JOHN ASH was born in Manchester in 1948 and read English at the University of Birmingham. He lived for a year in Cyprus, and in Manchester between 1970 and 1985, before moving to New York. Since 1996 he has lived in Istanbul. His poetry has appeared in many publications including the *New Yorker*, the *New York Times*, the *Village Voice*, *Oasis*, *PN Review* and *Paris Review*. Two of his Carcanet collections, *The Goodbyes* (1982) and *Disbelief* (1987) were Poetry Book Society Choices. He has also written two books about Turkey, *A Byzantine Journey* and *Turkey: The Other Guide*.

T0164294

Also by John Ash from Carcanet Press

The Goodbyes
The Branching Stairs
Disbelief
The Burnt Pages
Selected Poems
Two Books: The Anatolikon / To the City
The Parthian Stations

JOHN ASH

In the Wake of the Day

CARCANET

First published in Great Britain in 2010 by
Carcanet Press Limited
Alliance House
Cross Street
Manchester M2 7AQ

A CIP catalogue record for this book is available from the British Library
ISBN 978 1 84777 044 8

The publisher acknowledges financial assistance from Arts Council England

Typeset by XL Publishing Services, Tiverton
Printed and bound in England by SRP Ltd, Exeter

Contents

1 The Women of Kars

2 After Cavafy

3 The Bergamot Tree

Part 1

The Women of Kars

The Couple

When evening came on
The Great Wind started up,
And a knife flashed in the kitchen.

The old women were cowled
In white, sitting before doors so
Weathered their colour could not

Be determined. Black water thrashed.
Rain spattered down like bolts.
A vile stench issued from

The topiary bushes. The couple
On the far side of the wall spent
Whole evenings reciting numbers,

Then sealed themselves in their room.
Asphyxiation appeared
Inevitable, but they woke

Unharmed, and, in the calm
Of dawn, washed their clothes.

Olives

In the lands to the west of the Jordan
Olive groves were guarded by the soldiers of the kings
By night and day, and the destruction
Of a single tree was punishable by death
Or mutilation. This is no longer the case,
But I am not convinced of the improvement.

Unasked For

A white cloud came to the City,
Mouthing platitudes, contradictions,
And everything stopped,
Avenues silent as canals.

Lines of black statues carrying pistols
Appeared on the edges of the pavements.

I liked the embroidery and the gold,
But that was all. I placed flowers
In chapels (lilacs, peonies), but that
Was only because I didn't know what
I was doing, worshipping a tyranny.

Cloud of my childhood
And my mother's lukewarm prayers,
I do not understand this visitation.
You should be shut safely
In a nursery decorated by
A Renaissance master, one of the
More aimless ones, torn between
Faith and the apprehensible world
According to your dicta, which the day rejects.

I was an idiot like everyone else,
Neither ducking nor exceeding
The average level of malfeasance, I would
Have worshipped a cube, like the Nabataeans.
This might have been the more rational choice.

The late light on the sweet waters
Of this millennial harbour is a refutation
Worth a thousand volumes, a ton of inert icons.
I don't know what's happening, never have,
And *what*, in the words of the opera, *what*
Shall I do? The colours and the accents
Will change irrevocably. I have friends,

I think, but want no one beside me
Like a scented flank: that would be a disaster,
A paroxysm, lasting a lifetime and more.

This is precisely how it is.
You will learn nothing, absorbed as you are
By your white thoughts and the drowsing swans
Of your order. O emblems and symbols, return
At once to the absurd oval from which you came!

Finding Prostanna

for Bronwyn

On the way back
From the Canyon of Inscriptions,
I glimpsed for a second a sign that said
Prostanna, which I knew at once to be
A city of 'the wild Pisidians',
But there was no time that day
For further exploration, and we sped
Along the causeway to the island
(Weathered houses, metal-clad,
Plane trees, a boat builder hard at work,
Pensions, poppies, a small church like a barn).
As the light faded a fierce south wind sprang up,
And the white tablecloths were agitated
Like the wings of limed birds. We made
Enquires, and, yes, the waiters all agreed,
There was an ancient city called Prostanna.
It was easy to find. It was only five kilometres
Away, but they had told us what they thought
We wanted to hear, not anything they knew.
So, benignly misinformed, we set out
For Prostanna in the late afternoon
Of the following day, when, we reasoned,
The light would be at its most alchemical,
Turning stones to ingots. But what awaited us?
There might be a theatre perhaps? An agora,
Or a library, houses, towers, tombs, fine ashlar
Of the Hellenistic Period, when states quarrelled
Continually, but trade and cities flourished. All those
Antiochs, Alexandrias, Apameas and Seleucias…

The road wound up from the lake shore
Aslant a near-vertical mountainside.
Bronwyn winced, and moaned in the back seat,
Head down, and I said, perhaps a little callously:
'Well, dear, you wanted to see the Taurus Mountains…

And did you know that somewhere, I forget where,
Shakespeare alludes to *the snows of the Taurus*?'
We arrived, at last, on the edge of a natural terrace,
Suspended above the glass of the lake, and here
There was a village full of dark, wooden houses,
And a second sign proclaiming *Prostanna.*
This gave us hope, but the road ended, and the track
Branched and branched again, but signs remained,
Giving us further hope that the place could be
Reached, although our books were silent on the subject.
Tabula Rasa. Thus, it became inscribed and coloured
With images of which we had no knowledge or
True understanding. We walked for a long time,
Then everything began to seem uncertain. Flocks
Drifted across the slopes above us. We heard their bells,
But saw no sign of human artifice, not even
The clumsiest carving of an acanthus leaf or Ionic
Scroll, and advancing darkness menaced us.
We turned back, conscious of an exceptional failure.
The city was too far. We had been misled. But I
Did not excuse myself. Prostanna remained an idea,
Something like a thornbush or a cloud, blocking us.

In Jean Dubuffet's Crimson Landscape

The colours come to us
Pleading for acceptance. They come
In squares, which we perceive
As one side of a cube. There are more
Than a hundred of them, many more –
Amphora, Earth, Caviar, Amazon…
And I am obliged to choose, and choose
Only one, which will then surround me
For years like a landscape, inflecting,
Infecting each word I write, even
The humble swarms of articles,
Which, at present, all seem indefinite,
Though, given a choice, I favour the definite –
Solid like a tree centuries-old, giving
Shade to a tea-garden with a fountain.

In Jean Dubuffet's *Crimson Landscape*
There is a high horizon-line, above which
Is a saturated, inky blueness. Below it,
There are many deep, vermiform purples,
But, as I recall, nothing crimson or red.
Everything broods and simmers pleasingly
Like an active and fertile mind you would
Like to get to know better. In other places
On the pristine walls there are what may be
Humans, animals, or features of an invented
Geography, veiled under tones I cannot
Begin to define, which argues in favour
Of indirection and manifold ambiguities
Inscribed, perhaps, on vellum coloured a pale lilac,

But then the man in the green hat grins at you
Conspiratorially, hands on his hips;
The round figure in the red costume laughs out loud;
A blue woman embraces herself, swaddled,
Mummified, and you remain motionless, *in place*
Like a pillar in a pool of artificial light,

Or the celebrated circle of the lamp. You sit
On the bench of blond wood, beyond which it is
Best not to drift like a log or a raft of reeds.
Evening disturbs you (it is always this way),
And you are left, at last, in a world of loss,
Your mother gone, staring at blackened walls
Whose buried colours it is your task to uncover.

Babylon

Hear the flames now rising,
Their keen, exasperated rush,

Read their six thousand pages –
Flames of a heart, a fist, a liver, a lung,

Flames of dark, always dark (sad) eyes.
Don't ask, 'What is happening to

My pleasant civilisation with its many
Admirable markets and inventions,

This place like a park with fountains,
Boxwood avenues, and perspectives

Ending in long palisades of columns?'
Don't ask. It never existed, and you know it.

Remember the shattered windows of the stores,
The blood smeared on torn newspaper,

The smoke, and severed limbs underground,
The stench. Bilal, young, male, consigned

To some (yes) *godforsaken* periphery, said:
'We don't have the words, so we speak through fire.'

Blame lies elsewhere, like a lost cabinet,
In a Star Chamber, under the lush foliage

Of a stolen affluence, in desert places where,
Reversing history, uncounted people are sluiced

From ruined towns into camps without shade
Or water, and tank tracks are driven over Babylon.

Tristia

They planted trees on Music Street,
And how they've flourished,
Tossing their bright hair whenever
A breeze blows in from the Black Sea.

Then we recall the unforgiving
Emperor, Ovid's bitterness,
The nereids of Mandelstam...

★

Music blasts briefly from the stores,
Too loud and a little stupid like a drunk,
But I don't dislike it. Its energy
Irritates and infects. I edge

Forward through intervals of
Silence, albeit like a small boat
On a sea of uncertain temper.

★

Clouds pile up. The sun flashes.
Dust dims the street. Rain
Crashes down. The cat growls. Absurd,

All of it! But the tree that was cut
Almost to extinction has come back,
Shimmering, affording generous shade.

The past arrives much later
Like starlight, salt or poisoned water.

Near the Euphrates

In the market district
We admired the dried apricots.
It was a custom of the place,
Obligatory like a glass of tea.

The restaurant was octagonal
And surrounded by water.
The men from the town hall
Guffawed like lions.

The approach was guarded
By bronze busts of conquerors,
Frowning as if about to decide
The fate of a mutinous vassal.

Acacias were in purple bloom,
But snow still streaked the brown hills.
Tall brick columns rose like
Exclamations out of flourishing orchards,
And a boy showed me a ruinous
Mansion with a hooded hearth.

The narrow road twisted steeply
Down into hidden valleys.
Beyond them, beyond everything,
The great, tentacular river flashed
Like a mirror raised as a signal.

I felt then the exhilaration
Of a child released from the care
Of an anxious mother to spend a day
Wading in swift, clear streams, lips
Stained with the juice of mulberries.

But the memory is not mine, could not be…

Impossible

I was an impossible child. Why not
Admit it? I hated to be photographed,
Even though my father used a Leica
(The best available at the time).

I concealed myself in woods, among bushes
And brambles, emerging later with my new pants
Stained. On the summit of a mountain, I got lost
In fog. My mother trembled. I, of course, was

Perfectly OK. What was all the fuss about?
I was thin, but greedy. Given the chance, I ate
Whole jars of pickles, turned green and threw up.

Out of sheer perversity, I stamped on
A Roman Candle before its colours could explode.
Well, it wasn't a candle or Roman, was it?

I hated school. I hated sports. I hated the sea.
Most of all, I hated public swimming baths
Of the Edwardian era. I hated their smell,

And the pale, naked bodies of my classmates,
Which resembled rose-devouring grubs, but I
Thoroughly enjoyed thumping my sister on the head
With a heavy hard-backed book. Later,

I told my kind and sentimental English teacher
That Wordsworth wrote a poem about an idiot,
Because that was *what he was*. On

Another occasion I was so bad my mother
Fled the house to spend a night with her sister.
I ran after her along the dull, endless street,
Begging her to come home, which she did

On the following day. But what had I done?
It is an empty chalet by a loathsome lake.
I have no recollections of it, but fifty years on,

I haven't forgiven myself, or forgotten
The terror of her leaving. Most likely,
I broke something in anger, *a last straw*...

Poem: 'I never really wanted…'

I never really wanted
To put my thing into anything,
Or anyone. The prospect seemed
About as exciting as, say,
A logarithmic table, and I
Am not of a mathematical bent.

As to being fucked, well,
We all *are* in one way or another,

But perhaps this is no reason to
'Throw in the towel', and conclude
Prematurely that all of life is horrible.

It was not last time I checked.
The fan is open. You only have to choose
Which coloured spokes are yours, and what

They mean. But this raises more questions
As any thought, however crippled, must.
People are averse, and the answer might be nothing –

The vacant tomb of a nameless tyrant,
Hacked out of a cliff-face and unreachable.

Lines Written in a Hotel Room in Afyon

My name is ash.
No need to make
a big issue of that,

but it unnerves sometimes.
Some events or relationships
are said to *taste of ash*,

like the aftermath
of a medieval sack,
or worse, O much worse...

I am speaking of things
happening in my lifetime,
in my century (of which
I must take some sort
of possession, as if it were
a diary left idly open
on an escritoire by some
famous, political mother)

– incinerated cities,
hecatombs, the earth unable
to consume its corpses,
rivers filled with them and lakes...

But what am I to make
of any of this when
the only connection is
the coincidence of a name,
its horrible specifity.

My parents, meanwhile,
grew mad and died. I had hoped
that another meaning of the name
might gain authority,

that, under its sheltering influence,
they might be ushered out of life

in a style as orderly
as the way second subject
follows first in a prolonged
sonata movement by Mahler,
I wanted it to be endless,
and I wanted it cut off like a limb.

No chord was resolved,
yet it was *The Song of the Earth*
we listened to most often,
held motionless by the image
of friends meeting at evening
and parting forever: *ewig…*

The words were not sung,
no celesta accompanied them;
blue shadows did not descend
from the mountains, and birds
were silent as stones. What
you said at that last meeting was:
'Next time you come, I won't be here.'

I write this in a hotel room
in a town full of fountains,
and repugnant monuments
to the enmity of peoples, where I sit
trying not to forget anything at all.

The Cut

It is winter. Night is falling.
People rush home to turn on the lights.

The grid overloads. The power fails.
It is like this often. We shift and change,

Slipping to a poor, third place.
Inaudibly, a sigh goes up from kitchens

And bathrooms. No one thinks to protest:
'For five days it snowed, and now this...'

Candles flicker behind thin curtains.
The mother stops cooking, the painter

Drops his brush, the writer his pen;
In offices and homes the screens die;

Nor can the framer frame, or the welder weld:
There is nothing to do or be done.

Where does darkness lie? Ahead,
Behind? It does not end. Entire ages,

When knowledge lapsed, and emperors
Were proclaimed, then killed in an eyeblink,

Were named for it. Yet an interval opens
Like a fifth in music, though silent.

It would be wise to be calm, and we are,
Immersed, but attentive, acknowledging

What may happen without our consent,
While we remain motionless as obelisks

Until the light returns, and a river of
Incident flows again, and the weak craft

That carries us drifts ineluctably
Downstream to the expected destination.

Tramway

Sundown. The cannon sounds, and the call starts up,
But briefly, since everyone must attend to this evening's soup,
Which is essential to life. In truth, I barely register
These reports and acclamations, absorbed as I am in thoughts
Of the growing excellence of this city's public transportation,
Yet for fully nine years, I disdained it, as Tsarist nobles
Serfs, pre-emancipation, until my pockets emptied,
And the landscape changed. Scales fell. Now, I see how
Pleasantly the trams and buses move to and fro along
Their predestined routes, and whether they are green
Or blue, red or white, it is hard to resist the impulse
To jump on board – so jump – and sit back! There is
No need to argue with the driver, as sometimes happens
In a taxi: 'Where are you going? No, this is the wrong
Way. You have missed the turning. Stop at once,
You utter blockhead, I am getting out!' But on a bus,
Or a tram the driver knows exactly where he is going,
And so do you. There will be nothing improvisatory,
No anarchic detours in the style of Charles Ives.
He is devoted to an Idea of Order, which he may interpret
Ionically or ironically, since he is no one's slave.
He will get you there, wherever that might be, despite
Longeurs occasioned by the many private conveyances
People mysteriously persist in using, to our general
Detriment. This accords with nothing, as a harp concords
With a trombone. It is a crazed cult of individualism,
(In the Soviet sense of formalism), which you,
As an individual, can do nothing to eradicate,
So relax and look around. No one seems too ugly
Or unpleasant do they? Here, for example, is a group
Of five cheerful young people (students of music
I imagine). There are several empty seats, but they
Prefer to stand so they can talk and joke together.
And here are a girl and a boy, sound asleep, one
Slumped against the other. The bus lurches, and they wake
With a start, but are soon asleep once again. Evidently,
It has been a very long day for them. Then, for another

Instance, there is a woman who is so elegantly dressed
That you would expect to find her in a limousine,
But obviously she has more sense. Only a few feet away
Sits a handsome young man. He is neatly dressed,
And appears to be in the last stages of lassitude,
Which only makes him look more attractive.
Suddenly, his head tilts back, his eyes open like windows,
And he takes in his surroundings. He was, perhaps
Immersed in some profound reverie, but now he stands
To offer his seat to a much older foreign woman,
Who smiles gratefully. She also looks tired. It is the end
Of the day. We are all going home, and the soup is waiting.
It is made of lentils, garlic and spices. It warms the heart.
Meanwhile a mosque flashes by or appears to
(Its finials are gilded) then a second mosque, a third,
A drinking fountain, a palace and another palace, then
A second fountain with a beautiful inscription,
A tomb. Ancient planes make a vault above us.
We also pass many other buildings of ugly severity,
And some scrawny trees and shrubs, but the sea
Flashes, and the sun sets in glory, and it would be
Hard not feel a sense of gratitude for where we are,
And how, despite insuperable difficulties, we live –
Hard, also, not to recall the other meaning of *transported*.

Partial Explanation

What do I do? I look out the window
At the windows opposite and admire their keystones,
Which are adorned with fronds and scrolls, but am
Disappointed to observe that they are painted
An ugly shade of oxblood red. I sit in cafés
And read newspapers, giving them attention
I should probably expend on Homer, Shakespeare
Or the Upanishads. I am increasingly enamoured
Of my ignorance. I go to book stores,
But most times find nothing I wish to purchase.
I watch ink-blue clouds move in from the west.
I walk down a street to the *manav*, over
The broken cobbles, to buy vegetables of several
Vivid colours, and reflect happily that in
The dark Manchester of my youth none of these things
Could be found (they were a dream of the south
That could not be tasted), so perhaps circumstances
Have improved. Now, I live in a better climate
Fostering olives, vines and oleanders. When
A north wind blows I go south to a town called
'Eyebrow' because of the outline of a peninsula,
And friends live on this peninsula, and in a nearby bay
In beautiful houses. It is very pleasant to visit them,
But it is also pleasant to return to my home
In this imperial city without empire, place of paradox
And immemorial ambiguities where I work and sleep,
And here my chief duty is to care for the cat that came in
From the street, beloved creature, that speaks to me
With more than human eloquence, without complaint.

Practical Criticism

for Kenneth and Karen Koch

Again. Cigarettes, cigarettes, cigarettes.
We slip towards the edge of day, and over it.
Swoosh. Thud. Nearby, someone is playing a piano.

Great god! It may even be
A Forgotten Show Tune such as
No sane person would ever want to recall.

I ask you, is this anyway to celebrate
Or lament the advent of evening? Now comes
A florid arpeggio like syrup splashed

On a filthy, concrete floor, and he begins to sing
In a piercing, nasal whine, at least as attractive
As a dental drill. How can he be stopped,

So that evening can proceed, coolly descending
Parian steps? Electrify the piano, O Yamaha!
Or perhaps he should take a crash course

In the inimitable art of Bill Evans,
But I fear the undertaking would be hopeless –
Coffined melodies in all directions. The piano

Is a noble beast with strong sinews
Like the famous 'blood-sweating' horses
Of the Ferghana Valley, so prized by

The illustrious emperors of the Han dynasty
That they extended long miles of scarlet silk
To secure their purchase. And the piano

Is sensitive, of volatile temperament. Surely,
It cannot stand such punishment. It cannot.
Boom! It splinters with a sound like ice

Breaking on the Neva, beneath long,
Reflected façades, and yellow and black smoke,
Blooms from its metallic intestines. I see

The flames lick at the windows,
And the futile attempts to beat them back
With rugs and heavy curtains,

But it cannot be done. The piano is in a fury,
And the pianist is doomed, O let him perish
Along with several legions of bad poets

Who talk of underwear and dogs,
Muses, Moses and museums! He is silenced,
But so, sadly is the piano, which might have

Composed so exactly the various declensions
Of this strange evening of sunlight and heavy rain.
Kenneth would have said, if he had lived to see it –

What? Something about the stupendous copulations
Of prehistoric bats or giant fruits made of tufa.
Once, in Harry's glasshouse out on Long Island,

I said, for no particular reason: 'I can't stand
Chopin anymore.' You were shocked, taking me
Too seriously, but, Karen, I hadn't heard you play.

Difficult

Poetry is always difficult
Like a maladjusted child,
But perhaps it should only be
Difficult for the poet, not the reader.

This is a conclusion that increasingly
Appeals to me, but somehow,
Doesn't seem to curb my convolutions
And evasions, or the compelling impulse
To mention places no one has heard of.

Let us now consider with care the lost
Recital platforms of Sogdiana.

The Towel of Alyattes

Alyattes, king of Lydia, liked to bathe
In the gold-bearing waters of the River Pactolus,
And on emerging, would rub himself down
With a towel of purest white wool,
Which, over the years, became impregnated
With gold dust. The fame of the towel spread
Throughout the lands of western Asia,
But, on his death, it was found to have vanished.
He was known to have been very attached to it.
Had he taken it with him into the burial chamber
Beneath his great tumulus? Many thought so,
But over the decades and centuries their tunnels
Collapsed. So far, not a trace of the towel has turned up.

It is one of several, legendary, Anatolian
Textiles that have not come down to us.
How sad, how sheerly regrettable this is!
Among the greatest of them was the Covered Sheet
Of Lebissos, which remains wrapped in mystery.
We do not know what it was covered by
(Most likely a blanket or coverlet of some kind)
But it is known to have been gorgeously coloured,
And patterned, and may just have drifted off
Across the blue gulf in which it was created.

The Half-Mosque of Sivrishiar presents
No such problems. It can be plainly seen.
Work began in the mid-thirteenth century,
But the builders grew tired, and simply stopped.
It was just too big. But its curious a-
Symmetry has enchanted untold generations.

The Result

for Murat, Tolga, Nurseda, Eylül and Bahar

Perfectly formed water particles were falling
From clouds the colour of slate,
And sinister young girls were singing

In walled gardens between banks
Of roses that urge purity,
But cannot accomplish innocence.

Exfoliate, they know too much about
History and sexuality, as these things
Might appear to us in colours we don't own,

And the green lizard flickering in the apse
Of the Red Church is an ornament
For a wrist that does not yet exist.

I break against hope (time and again),
I break mirrors to review the revised
Reflection: a formal oval of still water

On which the name of a vanquished sister
Cannot be inscribed. The roses
Always return, but are over too soon,

Before summer has set its measured pace,
Rotting on Nicene frames. A bitter fountain
Rises, hot and salt, towards the marble brow

Of whoever may be chosen for this moment
Due to their blankness or beauty. It is right
That the exceptional should be raised

To the heavens like the lock of Berenice
Constellated by Callimachos. Surely,
There is nothing to fear from the rain that falls

Generously into our narrow divisions.
I possess all that I need: instruments, streets,
The passionate voices of women,

And what is here, close as an embrace.

The Women of Kars
(or Some Other Places I Know and Do Not Know)

I have not been to Mardin, which everyone praises.
Its houses of honey-coloured stone gaze out
Over the immense, Mesopotamian plain –
An ocean of earth that seems to swim in the light.
Nor have I seen the shattered bridge of Hasankeyf,
Capital of the illustrious Artukid princes,
Which may soon be drowned. I had better hurry.
It is already too late for Zeugma and Samosata.
Then there is Abrahamic Urfa, seat
Of the Abgarid kings, with its cave, and pools
Stocked with sacred carp. When will I get there,
And what is the best time to pay a visit? Harran,
Once a great centre of learning, lies nearby.
Deep into the Middle Ages it remained
The principal cult-centre of the Sabians, pagans
Who worshipped the sun and the moon, and believed
All matter to be inherently evil (and here, also,
Socrates and Plato were revered as intellectual gods,
And impassioned symposia were held). All of these things
Make me want to go to these places immediately.
Sadly, this is not possible, but I *have* been to Kars.

My reasons for going there were diverse,
But not especially complex: 1, it had been
Described in a guidebook as 'possibly
The most depressing town in Turkey', but I knew
The authors of this volume to be invincibly
Condescending, and so concluded that Kars might be
Altogether delightful; 2, the people in my
Corner store are from Kars, and they are unfailingly
Courteous; 3, the novelist Orhan Pamuk
Had just published an enigmatic and troubling book
Called *Kar*, which means *snow* in Turkish,
And the action takes place, as one might expect,
In Kars during a snowstorm. The town, in his account,
Is certainly depressing, but enlivened by the presence

Of several beautiful women; 4, I found myself
In the small town of Shavshat, which is only
A few hours distant from Kars, and there seemed
No good reason not to go. It was a journey
Of extreme beauty and desolation. The bus struggled,
Creaking and grinding, first climbing through
Bright, alpine meadows on which handsome
Wooden houses with window boxes were disposed
In a manner recalling the better aspects of Switzerland.
Then, in a moment, everything changed utterly. On
The summit of the pass, the trees vanished,
And did not return. The houses of the villages seemed
Sunk into the earth, and were so overgrown with grasses,
They resembled burial mounds. Were those I saw
In the streets ghosts? Exhausted, I arrived in Kars,
And found it both exemplary and anomalous. How
Could it not be, given its peculiar history? Trees
Lined the grid Russians had built in the image
Of Tsarist order (and perhaps, also, they were
A little homesick in this wild place, so far
From the Neva and the façades of their palaces).
Feeling somewhat bewildered, a not unpleasant
Sensation when one has just arrived in
An interesting place, I stopped to ask directions
Outside a mobile phone store. At once,
A young man rushed out and exclaimed:
'What are you looking for? I can help you!'
He was a student of literature. Had he read *Kar*?
No, but his friends had, and they didn't like it. They said:
'Kars is not like that. We are not like that.'
But perhaps they were wrong. He would decide for himself.
Then he asked: 'What do you think of Kars?'
And I said that it seemed like a very pleasant town.
Why did people say it was depressing? 'Yes,' he said
Pensively, 'in the summer it is nice, but the winters
Are long and very cold. Then there are the wolves…'
'Wolves!' I incredulously interjected. 'Yes,'
He mildly continued, 'when the snow is deep,
They come down from the hills to look for food.'
I asked: 'Aren't they dangerous?' And he replied:

'Oh, not really. If you find some wolves in your garden,
you just call the police. Usually they run away.'
Usually? I wondered what might occur in
Unusual circumstances. Such are the illuminating
Conversations one engages in on the streets of Kars.

My new friend recommended a hotel,
Which I liked at once, despite the manager's air
Of bearded despondency, which brought to mind
The moralisings of Alexander Solzhenitsyn.
I set out for the Church of the Holy Apostles,
Which was massive, black, and of a tetraconch
Design. Now it is a mosque, which is certainly better
Than it being a locked warehouse or barn,
And how great is the difference for the irreligious?
Both creeds are, after all monotheistic,
Though Christianity has muddied the issue
Somewhat with its strange doctrine of the Trinity.
These things cannot be countenanced for very long,
Or our lives would end in confusion and
Superstition (votive rags tied to trees,
Murdered dogs buried at crossroads)
With only the phantasmal hope of a life
Beyond life to sustain us like a rail
To grasp as we grow physically impaired,
And start to talk to people who don't exist,
Or exist only in memory or antique fictions –
Beautiful, treacherous, heroic, betrayed…

A great brown river roared by.
I had not expected such energy and velocity
In a place I had imagined as lost in distance
And torpor like an inscription in cuneiform,
Which the custodian will translate for you
Into another language you also do not
Understand. The possible recessions
And declensions are almost infinite,
Incomputable. So, instructed by what I saw,
I walked beside the river, which turned east,
Around a grim fortress to join the Akhurian,

Which then led south to the Araxes, all
These turbulent waters debouching at last
Into the Caspian amid rotting oil rigs,
And soon I came to streets of elegant houses,
And a park where an artificial waterfall
Plunged voluminously down a real rock face.
I was reminded of a similar waterfall
In the down of Kastamonu, hereditary fief
Of the Comnenian emperors, and I thought
Of how many stories these towns have to tell.
Next to the waterfall was a restaurant
Where I paused for a raki accompanied, as
Tradition demanded, by melon and white cheese.
The waiter was so welcoming, that, within seconds,
I felt as if I had known him for years. I began
To make my way back to the hotel, passing
Prodigious numbers of stores selling honey
And cheeses (for which Kars is famous)
But instead of honey or cheese, I bought socks
As is my custom when visiting Turkish towns.
In Antakya the socks were olive green,
In Egridir blue, in Kars cream and grey.

I was almost at the hotel, where
I would be protected from alcohol
And irrational purchases, when I saw
A sign proclaiming PLANET BAR.
I could not resist. I stepped inside,
And fell instantly in love. It was
Not only a bar, but a fast food outlet,
And a shabby patisserie with empty shelves.
It was cavernous, gloomy and empty,
Apart from a group of men in ill-fitting suits
Drinking tea in a corner. At once they were
My brethren. I sank down gratefully
On a lumpy red banquette and ordered
A second raki. There is a paradoxical comfort
In Turkish gloom, in which you can wrap yourself
As in a thick soft blanket, and lie down
(Psychologically speaking) knowing that

All the aggravating things you have to do
Tomorrow or the next day are meaningless,
Because life is sad, fundamentally so,
And the songs go on like roads or rivers
In minor keys, and are shared by others
In other places of which you have no knowledge.

When, at last, I entered the hotel lobby,
I was greeted by a short man with bright,
Intelligent eyes, who introduced himself as Celil
And asked: 'Do you want to go to Ani?'
For more than forty years I had wanted to go to Ani,
Splendid capital of the Bagratid Kingdom, proud
Seat of kings named Ashot, Smbat and Gagik,
But many obstacles had intervened
Like poverty, or the fact of living in England
Or America, so far from what lured me. It seemed
That I lived in a permanent state of suspension,
Always hoping that I might arrive *there*,
Wherever that might be (Ani being but one
Instance). I fell asleep thinking of towers,
Of finely cut red and black stone, fallen
Vaults, and the origins of styles we name
Too confidently, for our arrogance breaks
Beyond all bounds, then I woke and went.
I was not disappointed. The great fragments
Rose from long grasses above the deep gorge
Of the Akhurian. It seemed a city
At the world's edge. All the while there was
A faint whistling or sighing as if the wind passed
Through a stack of bones, bleached and forgotten,
And the grinding of machines, wounding the landscape.
The mosque was not a mosque, but a pavilion
Attached to a palace, a cool retreat
For summer days, and here young soldiers
Casually patrolled, and under red vaults
A banquet was being prepared, but for whom
Was unclear, except that they had the power
To command such a place. Small birds flew
In and out of the cathedral's opened O, and here

Early travellers saw a prefiguring of gothic
In composite piers and softly ogival arches,
But perhaps something more than mere accident
Pertains, for, in Antioch, when it was ruled
By barbarian princes from the west, there were
Many Armenians, who were considered to be
The most skilful stonemasons of that time.
Without them the walls of Cairo would not stand,
Nor those of Amida, which we call by another name.

On our way back to Kars, Celil spoke with
Deep affection of his Armenian grandmother
Who spoke fluent Russian, and, during a long
And dignified life, never knew a day's ill-health,
Regarding all modern prescriptions with perfect disdain,
And I thought of a photograph of the women of Kars,
Taken, I believe, at some time shortly before 1921,
Which I had found one humid and oppressive
Summer afternoon in an obscure New York
Library. Magnificent in long, dark robes, veils,
And gold diadems with pendants, they resembled
Heroines from the age of Agamemnon.

Part 2

After Cavafy

Without Memorial

The son of a poor sailor from the Aegean,
He worked for the blacksmith. His clothes
Were threadbare, his shoes scuffed and cracked,
His hands calloused, ingrained with dust and oil.

In the evenings, after the shop had closed,
If there was something he longed to possess –
An expensive tie to wear on Sundays, or
A deep blue shirt he'd glimpsed in a window –
Then he would sell himself for a couple of pounds.

I ask myself if, in the days of Alexandria's glory,
There was ever a youth more perfectly handsome
Than this one life threw aside without memorial,
For, of course, no portrait exists, no statue or painting…

Cast into the abyss of the blacksmith's, caught between
Brutal labour and common debauchery, he was destroyed.

Fever of Kleitos

1

Kleitos, a young man well-liked by all,
And some twenty-three years of age,
Son of a distinguished family, possessed
Of a refined knowledge of the Greek classics,
Has fallen desperately ill. The fever that ravaged
Alexandria this year has found him out –

Has found him already weakened by despair,
Knowing that the young actor he doted on
No longer desires him, no longer wants him around.

His condition is critical.
His terrified parents don't know where to turn.

An old maidservant, who helped raise him,
Also trembles with fear. In her agitation,
She suddenly recalls an idol she worshipped
As a child before she came as a servant
To this noble household of Christians,
And herself became a Christian. In secret,
She bakes votive breads, brings wine and honey,
And sets them before the idol. In no particular order,
She mumbles fragments of hymns and prayers,
Dimly remembered, not realising, poor fool,
That to her little black demon, whether a Christian
Lives or dies is a matter of complete indifference.

2

They say Kleitos asked for me on his deathbed.
I was touched, of course, but did not go.
Only a fool would have done so. The fever
That killed him was fiercely contagious,
And my love for him had died some months before.
Someone came along who excited me more.

True, the Gods can be cruel sometimes,
But how can I be blamed for that?

Nor did I attend the funeral,
He was a Christian after all,
And I cannot abide the religion, besides
His family might not have allowed it.
One thing I could do for him without risk,
Without betraying my deepest convictions –
Place flowers on his grave, jasmine and roses.

The Battle of Magnesia

1 A Maker of Mixing Bowls

On this fine mixing bowl of pure silver,
Made for the house of Heraclides

(Renowned for its discerning taste),
I have set the most elegant flowers, sprigs

Of thyme, and a flowing stream from which
A handsome youth, nude and amorous,

Is just emerging. I have prayed, O Mnemosyne,
For your guidance so that I might portray

The face of the young man I once loved
As it used to be, but it has been hard;

Nearly fifteen years have passed since he
Fell, a soldier on the field of Magnesia.

2 Sorrow of Macedon

He has quite lost his old fire and vigour.
His limbs tremble, he can hardly raise a sword.

From now on he'll set all ambition aside,
Or so he, Phillip, King of Macedon, maintains.

He's had enough of disputes and defeats. In all
His battles, what was he fighting for? Tonight

He'll play dice and drink deep, so let the table
Be strewn with roses, many roses...

If Antiochus was utterly vanquished
At Magnesia what does it matter to him?

It's said that his entire, splendid army was slaughtered,
But surely it cannot be true, pray God it is not true,

And these are merely wild rumours, But one 'Pray God'
Is perhaps enough. The banquet will not be put off.

Bring roses. If his body begins to fail him
His memory is clear: he remembers how deeply they mourned

In Syria when Macedon, their mother, was trampled in the dirt.
So tonight he'll drink deep. Bring slaves, flutes and torches.

Antiochus Epiphanes

A young man of Antioch addressed the Great King:
'My heart is filled with a long-cherished hope.
Once again the Macedonians, Antiochus Epiphanes,
The Macedonians, I say, have resumed the noble contest.

If it would ensure their victory, I'd gladly give away
The lion and the horses, the coral statuette of Pan,
The luxurious villa, the Tyrian gardens, and all the gifts
You've showered on me, Antiochus Epiphanes.'

For a moment the king may have been touched,
But he recalled the fates of his father and brother,
And said nothing. Someone might be listening,
Might repeat certain compromising words. Besides,
The inevitable reckoning followed shortly at Pydna.

The Gods in their Wisdom

Antioch, you'll be the death of me.
I'm nearly penniless, and before long
I'll be evicted, thrown into a stinking gutter,
And it's you who are to blame, fatal,
Extravagant, whorish city of Antioch!

Then again, I'm still young, in good health,
And not bad-looking, and my mastery of Greek
Is second to none. I know Plato and Euripides,
Backwards, and orators, sophists *ad libitum*
Nor am I entirely ignorant of military affairs:
I count some of the mercenary chiefs among my friends.
Even in government circles, I have a foot in the door,
And last year I spent six months in Alexandria,
So I know a thing or two about the place that could
Be useful: the depravities of Kakergetes, and so on...

In sum, I consider myself eminently qualified
To serve my native country, beloved land of Syria!

In whatever position I'm placed, I'll strive to act
For the general good. That at least, is my sincere intention.
If, however, they thwart me with their intrigues
(You know the kind of creatures I'm speaking of)
If, as I said, they thwart me, it is none of my doing.

Firstly, I'll apply to Zabinas,
But, if that blockhead doesn't recognise my talents,
I'll turn to his rival Grypos, and if that numbskull
Won't offer me a place, I'll go immediately to Hyrcanos.

I'm confident one of them will take me on.
The fact that I don't give a damn which one it is
Doesn't trouble me. My conscience is clear, since
All three of the sons-of-bitches are equally bad
For Syria. I'm down on my luck, what else can I do?

The Gods in their wisdom might have taken the time
To produce a fourth man who was upright and honest.
To him I would gladly have pledged my allegiance.

In Ösroene

Last night, about midnight, they brought back
Our friend Rhemon, wounded in a drunken brawl.

Through the open window moonlight illumined
The bed, and the complete perfection of his body.

We're a mixed bunch here – Syrian, Greek,
Persian, Armenian – and Rhemon is no exception,

But, last night, as we looked at him in the moonlight,
We could think of nothing, of no one but Plato's Charmides.

Disillusionment of Demetrius Soter

All his hopes came to nothing.

Once he dreamt of performing wonders,
Of lifting the weight that had pressed his people
Down in the years that had followed Magnesia,
Dreamt that he would bring glory back to Syria –
Syria with her armies, and numberless ships,
Her strong citadels, and vast wealth…

In Rome he suffered, and grew bitter,
Sensing in the talk of his erstwhile friends –
All young people of good families –
Despite the discretion and courtesy
They always showed towards him, the son
Of Seleucus Philopator, an underlying
Contempt for the Hellenistic dynasties:
They had declined, they were impotent,
They could no longer be taken seriously.
In anger, he shut himself away, and swore
That things would turn out differently.

And why shouldn't it be so? He had courage,
And a strong resolve. His actions would surely
Inspire the people to rise up, to exalt themselves –
If only, if only he could find some way to escape
Italy, and return, at last, to his homeland. Ah Syria!…
But did he really know the place? When he was taken,
A hostage to ensure his father's good behaviour,
He had been a child. He could barely remember
How it looked, but had always thought of it
With reverence and longing as a radiant vision
Of Greek cities, and Greek harbours. But now?

Now, there is nothing but misery and despair.
These smug, young people in Rome were right after all:
The dynasties that Alexander's conquests brought
Into being are wholly incapable, finished…

He tells himself it doesn't matter. He gathered
All his energy, and did his best. He fought against the odds.
He failed, but through it all displayed his courage,
As was appropriate to the son of Seleucus Philopator.

His whole project began in dreams and ended in futility.
The Syria he imagined is nowhere to be found
In this alien land of conspirators and usurpers.
Let them take it, the damnable Heracleides and Balas.

The Triumph of John Kantakouzenos

1   A Bishop's Assurances

He gazes on the fields he can still call his own –
On the fields of wheat, the cattle, the flourishing orchards,
And beyond them he sees his ancestral home,
Filled with fine clothing, costly furnishings, silverware.

Soon it will all be taken from him. O God, it will be taken…

Perhaps, if he threw himself at his feet
Kantakouzenos would take pity on him. He is not,
After all, a vindictive man, no, not at all vindictive.
But his followers? And his army? No, it would be better
To prostrate himself before his noble wife, the Lady Irene.

What a fool he had been to join the Empress Anna's party,
And would that Lord Andronikos had never married the woman.
Consumed with suspicion, believing anything she was told,
What good has she ever done? When has she revealed
The slightest sign of compassion or understanding?

Why even the Franks (and she's one of them)
Regard her with contempt. Her scheming was absurd,
All her plotting ended in farce. Safe, as they thought,
Behind the walls of the City, they blustered and menaced
Until the Lord John outmanoeuvred them completely.

And to think that it had been his first thought
To join John's party! If he had done so he would be rejoicing now –
A great nobleman securely established on the winning side,
But he had listened to that confounded bishop, who, it turned out,

Had been wrong from beginning to end, whose suave assurances,
And priestly rhetoric were no more than a sorry collection of idiocies.

2 Of Coloured Glass

There is one thing that saddens me deeply
Concerning the coronation at Blachernae
Of John Kantakouzenos and Irene,
Daughter of Andronikos Asen, that they lacked
Precious stones (such was the poverty of the state
In its decline) and their crowns were inlaid
With many small pieces of coloured glass –

Red, green and blue. But I do not see in this either
Indignity or humiliation, rather, they appear to me
(These scintillas of cheap glass)
As a sorrowful protest against the undeserved
Afflictions of those who must wear them, representing
Everything that is missing (purloined and pawned)
And should have been the due of John Kantakouzenos
And the daughter of Tsar Andronikos on their coronation day.

Exiles

True, it has suffered, but Alexandria
Remains Alexandria. Walk but a short way
Along the straight road to the stadium,
And you'll see monuments that will amaze you.
Whatever it has suffered, however much
It is diminished, it is still a great city.
And what with excursions, books and our studies
We pass the time pleasantly. In the evenings,
We gather on the waterfront, the five of us,
Together with some of the few Greeks who remain.
Sometimes we discuss ecclesiastical matters,
Sometimes literature: only the other day we read
Verses by the celebrated Nonnos of Panopolis –
What images, what rhythms and harmonies!...
So the days pass by agreeably enough,
And we remind ourselves we won't be here for long.
There's very promising news from Smyrna,
And in April our allies will set out from Epirus.
Without doubt, our schemes are proceeding admirably,
And soon we'll make short work of the usurper Basil –
That son of slaves who calls himself emperor...

A Byzantine Nobleman Writing in Exile

It is only the frivolous who call me frivolous.
I have always been very diligent in my readings
Of the Cappadocian Fathers, the Scriptures
And the Synodical Canons. Whenever
He was in doubt, whenever there was
Some problem concerning church affairs
The Emperor Nikephoros Botaneiates
Always turned to me first of all. But now,
In exile (may that viper, Irene Doukas,
Rot in Hell for it), and quite appallingly bored,
It isn't at all strange that I should choose
To divert myself with sestets and octets
Praising Apollo, Hermes, and Dionysos
Or the heroes of Thessaly and the Peloponnese
In impeccable iambics, which the poets of the capital
Cannot begin to rival. It is this very perfection that –
If I may hazard a guess – makes them traduce me so.

In a Syrian Harbour

He arrived in this small Syrian harbour
With plans to take up the trade in incense,
But during the voyage he had fallen ill,
And, almost as soon as he was brought ashore,
He died. We buried him. It was the poorest burial.
We knew his name was Emes and that he was young.
That was all. Just before dying, he muttered
Something about 'home' and 'parents',
But who they might be no one knew, nor which corner
Of this immense, Hellenic world of ours
He could call home, and perhaps it is better so:
Although he lies buried in this insignificant
Harbour-town, his parents will never learn of it,
And can live on the hope that one day he'll return.

Part 3

The Bergamot Tree

Pinara

As the strong afternoon breeze
Emerged, severely predictable,
From the ravine the pines sighed
And moaned, and the shadow of the mountain
Engulfed everything but the theatre,
My American friend shivered and said:
'I feel like an intruder. I shouldn't be here.'
But across the valley, the arches of a bath
Still blazed with light under
The rose-coloured peaks of the White Mountains.
O omens, consolations and Hittite correspondences,
What are we to make of these fragments,
These hisses and whispers? Who were
These people who were buried in uncounted chambers
Hacked into the sheer side of a precipice,
Which in their extinct language, they called 'round',
Which it was not, great wall of sorrow and forgetting.
They were perhaps, undistinguished by the standards
Of their time, producing no poets or philosophers
Whose names history has recorded, but they lived.

In the Wake of the Day

I want to get drunk to write so much that
I no longer know what I'm thinking and fall darkly asleep.
(I don't care if I dream or not.) I don't want to be depressed,
Or tired or a saint, or even a sage (what a responsibility!),
And certainly not a siege with castled elephants and catapults.
I'd like to go and look at some ruins I haven't seen before.
That would be puzzling and refreshing as all things should be.
O colonnades, basilicas and cisterns! I don't want to go to
The supermarket, the movies, Paris, America or Lapland.
Who would want to be encumbered with reindeer and their bells?
I want to read a book on some enormous, inscrutable topic
Like *The Origins of the Pendentive* or *Sassanian Jurisprudence*,
But I refuse to go to the bookstore, which always confuses me.
I mean, how do you find anything in there? I want to run around
And meet new people, but at the same time, the very idea
Of leaving this room appals me completely. (It is a strange
Ottoman hexagon with a window-alcove that delights me.)
And how can any erudite, good-humoured adult of the kind
You would like to meet be 'new' in any meaningful sense?

I don't want to do anything. I want to be everything –
A composer of coruscating scherzos and neurotic adagios,
Or the captain of a very large ship in an Alaskan fiord, or
A stoat, a rock, a swan, or just a contented goat asleep
On the road in front of a bus-load of tourists, who are
Desperate to see the waterfalls and the eternal fire.
I wouldn't want to be a mosquito, perpetually whining,
Or a literary critic detested by all. After all, what do they know
That isn't blindingly obvious like a slab of rock-salt
Landing on your head from an impressive height? A lizard
Would also be OK, I think, especially if it was viridescent,
And had a discriminating taste for Byzantine architecture.
In the case of the captain, I'm sure the uniform, whether white
Or blue, would look very stylish. The trouble is I hate the sea.
Why does it have to surge and swell so like a romantic poem
Of imponderable banality? I don't want to be Swinburne

Or a pornographer do I? Gloop, gloop. And I don't want to be
Rich or poor. I just want to have enough and no more.

I don't want the 'don't wants' to exceed the 'wants' in this poem,
But they do, as the inhabitants of Istanbul easily outnumber
All the people of Kazakhstan & Kyrgyzstan taken together. The city
Is too big for the mind to encompass in a lifetime, or at all,
Though the attempt must be made, and I certainly have no plans
To leave; an era of investigations lies ahead of me like a rolling steppe
Ending at high, clouded mountains. And where would I go?
Oslo? I don't want evening to come on so early (it is late November),
But I love twilight and rain for no obvious reason other
Than that they seem to embody an impersonal memory beneath
Whose vast, semicircular terraces The Opera of the Orient
Is staged in splendour amid the speech of cymbals and ouds,
To appease a fractious pasha. But there is a misunderstanding here,
A palimpsestic overlay of dubious assumptions, and how am I
To get to the root of it all? I am not a critic or a philosopher,
Nor would want to be. Nor am I Rameau or Mozart, much as I
Would like to be, and the river (which is not a river) pursues its
Course with turbulence, and something that seems like knowledge.

Finding Prostanna (2)

A storm was circling above the blue glass of the lake.
The driver was worried. Would I be safe on the mountain
In such uncertain weather? I reassured him,
Telling him not to wait, and began the long ascent.
The wind blew cold, and I was not dressed for the event,
Taking frequent refuge under pines that offered
Scant shelter from drenching blasts of rain. Again,
It seemed as if I would be blocked in the midst of my search.
There were many springs still flowing although it was
Already late summer, and this, I thought, explained
How a city could have been established in such
Isolation, at such a prodigious elevation. I met
A man descending in a fury of frustration,
Having spent hours trying to find the place, but failing:
'There are all those stupid signs,' he exclaimed,
'But when you really need one there's nothing.' This
I knew, but I continued to climb, now more wearily.
Before me lay an allegory of defeat. There was also
The perplexing question of why I wanted to find the city
When I had been unable to unearth anything about it,
Other than that it had a name, was ancient, and lay nearby.
Prostanna had become a myth, but one only
Of my own making, and likely to flicker out of existence
At any moment like a doused flame. I was, I think,
Mildly obsessed, which seemed not only harmless, but correct:
These cities must be found and acknowledged. We must think
Of why people lived in them (the tedium of trade, resources,
Politics). These explanations are never convincing.
Was it rather an attachment to a place, a landscape,
A setting of exceptional beauty, in which case the act of foundation
Was an act of love, at once imponderable, and as easy
To understand as a child's birthday party. Yet,
The questions 'Why here?' 'Why there?' continue to
Irritate like an eczema, and we are at a loss, as so often,
Questioning our knowledge. It is possible to uncover
An entire city, but, without inscriptions, to know nothing
Of its history or customs, unless, as at Kanesh, the Assyrians

Left records of trade on cuneiform tablets. Otherwise, nothing but
Mud, stones, hearths, sherds, the vanished fumes of families,
Their excrement and saliva. I walked to the summit
Of a sharp ridge, but saw only the peak of Mount Davras,
And the long, straight road to Isparta. Dispirited,
I began my descent along the sodden track through clay
That stuck fast to shoes. Soon, I was barely able to walk. Then,
I happened to glance to my left, through the skeleton
Of a pylon, and saw, in the mid-distance, what might
Have been a rock-formation, but seemed too ordered
And regular. I moved towards it through fields of long grass,
And, in what seemed no more than a moment, found myself
Walking along the terraces and ramparts of Prostanna.
I was *there*, but somehow the city still eluded me:
On every side there were mounds of fine, ashlar masonry,
But nothing recognisable as a temple, church or house.
It was all formless, indeterminate, lost (though found).
There is much more to be said on this subject of which this
Is a mere fragment: *I count myself not to have apprehended.*

Two Poems with an Uncritical Apparatus

To Describe an Evening

Can it be done, when it surrounds you
Like a tent of grey silk? Rain has washed
The façades. Between buildings and beyond
Lines of washing, a weak silver sunset
Is visible, but the length of evening is
Behind me, beginning as a nest of shadows
In the Altay Mountains. Its wings beat slowly
As it passes over Merv and Hecatompylos,[1]
But evening is only a marker, and this evening,
After so much rain, is undeniably dull,
A damaged watercolour, but how much I love
The word, and the world it contains: *abend, akşam...*

It is best interpreted by music.
A cassation, a serenade, it *is* music.

Further to the Above

What is music and what does it mean?
I suppose it must have begun with a punk clashing
Of sticks and stones, chants perhaps, and echolalia.
But I talk constantly as if it were a universal blessing,
When (let's face it) some of it is unspeakably bad,
Wagner, for example. And imagine a world
That could only be accurately expressed through
Heavy Metal or Gothic, and the accompanying
Teenage suicides. Don't. It is too horrible
To contemplate. You might as well be deaf,
And spend the rest of your life in a small toilet
With shit-stained wallpaper, where you would
Certainly not be joined by Luther Vandross, Alicia Keys,
Marvin Gaye, Webern or Alexander Von Zemlinsky,[2]

★1   Where is Merv? Who knows or cares?
It was once vast, stretching from horizon
To horizon, its endless walls enclosing
Verdant oases. It lay in Khorasan and was
The chief city of that region. Once. Now, amid
The fields of rubble nothing grows save tamarisks,
Dwarf acacias, and the shrub known as saxaul,
Or *Anabasis ammodenaron*. Figurines
Have been unearthed, one showing a man
With an erect penis, a second a woman holding up
A mirror, a third (made of glass) another woman
In 'the birthing position'. Beyond the walls
Of Merv, Sultan Sanjar built for himself
A prodigious domed tomb. He wished to be remembered,
As a ruler of benevolence and wisdom.
The restless tribes paid him homage. His domains
Stretched from the Jaxartes to the Indian Ocean.
Then, in eyeblink (a revolt of his own Ghuzz kinsmen),
He was destroyed. In the present town of Merv,
The only hotel amid the dull, begrimed grid
Of streets makes the heart sink, and water fills
The basement of the museum. O Merv!
Your walls still stand to a height of over sixty feet.
As to Hecatompylos,★3 where the empire
Of the Parthians had its beginnings, we have no
Clear idea of its location. Damghan is a possibility.

★2   Alexander Von Zemlinsky felt that he was deeply ugly and dwarfish.★4 It did not help that he was a Galician Jew living in Vienna. It did not help that he fell in love with his beautiful, gifted, and immoderately vain student, Alma Schindler,★5 who rebuffed him and married Gustav Mahler. It did not help that he regarded Mahler as a god among men, as did his brother-in-law Arnold Schoenberg who, towards the end of his life, remarked of Zemlinsky: 'I have always considered him to be a great composer, and I still do.' It did not help. He ended his days forgotten in Westchester County, writing songs no one performed. How could this have happened? Happily, the story does not end here, for at a point, some thirty years after his death, the realisation gradually dawned that Schoenberg had been right all along. How could this loss, this wilful ignorance have been sustained? It should not have happened. The story turned. It was discovered that his operas were magnificent, his songs and string quartets likewise. How, to cite just one instance, can anyone hear the great barcarolle from the Fourth Quartet without dashing streams of tears from their eyes? Unless you happened to be tone deaf and heartless, it is impossible, even if you do not know the circumstance in which it was written, in Berlin under the encroaching cloud of a nightmare. It did not help. It should not have happened, and we are left with this great beauty and exquisite craft given to us by a man who thought himself hideous, the dwarf in Oscar Wilde's *Birthday of the Infanta,* who shattered and died on seeing himself in a mirror.

★3   The name Hecatompylos must be related to the word 'hecatomb', which originally meant a sacrifice of a hundred oxen, but has since come to mean any mass slaughter, whether of animals or humans. In theory, it could have been applied to Cambodia or Rwanda, but it was not. For the Parthians, evidently, it had no negative connotations, and their first capital must have been a holy city where, it can be presumed, sacrifices of an extravagant order were made to the many and diverse gods of their obscure pantheon, which included, most unusually, a male, lunar deity. The word can also mean a perfect measure of a hundred units. This sounds Roman and orderly, suiting our prejudices, but the Parthians were Iranian, and of nomadic origins.

★4   It is a curious fact that many of the twentieth century's greatest composers were extremely short, among them Mahler, Schoenberg, Stravinsky and Webern. Alban Berg (see below) loomed over them all.

★5   Schindler also had an affair with the painter Oskar Kokoschka. She is portrayed, wrapped in his arms, in the painting known variously as *The Tempest* or *The Bride of the Winds,* but she did not marry him. Instead, after the premature death of Mahler, she chose the architect Walter Gropius, and soon gave birth to a daughter whose death at the age of seventeen inspired Berg to write his Violin Concerto, which is inscribed 'To the memory of an angel'. The poor girl was named Manon after sentimental operas by Massenet and Puccini. She deserved better, which is what Berg gave her in the form of variations on a Bach chorale. Then, shortly after, he too died of a septic bee-sting. In his Lyric Suite Berg quotes a melody from Zemlinsky's Lyric Symphony. Both works are cast in six movements. There is a pattern here if only it could be found.

Stations

for K.K. in memory

My friend disappointed me.
At the last minute he changed his mind:
He would not be making the journey with me
After all. A better option had turned up.
I didn't appreciate it, but thought: 'What the hell,
I'll go anyway, even without a car.' And I did,
Taking your obituary with me, and signed
Copies of *Straits* and *New Addresses*,
I crossed the Sea of Marmara without incident,
Passing the islands of exile along the way,
And jumped on a bus (sleek and too slow)
That deposited me in an *otogar* painted
Pink and grey, where there were whole drifts
And waves of weeping women, and handsome
Young men taking their leave of them, and their friends,
Who embraced them fiercely as if they feared
They might never return. And water was poured
On the ground behind the departing buses,
Several of which were emblazoned with designs
Resembling the paintings of Kasimir Malevich.
A libation! Such was the custom: tears, water,
Valediction. I was touched, but puzzled, since
I wasn't convinced that all of these people
Were impassioned admirers of your work,
Though it was pleasant to entertain the idea.
A long mountain loomed ahead, seemingly
Uncircumventable, but we turned east into
A narrow, forested valley that led up by degrees
To the great, bald pate of the plateau, and its cities,
Which unseasonal rainstorms lashed.
It was a scene very different from your house
Amid the Long Island potato fields, where
I was your guest one blistering August (O
Dinner-parties, and endless, monotonous beaches!)
The next station was coloured purple and yellow,
And here there were more weeping women, and more

Passionate farewells: tears, rain, departures…
Then I understood. It was the time of conscription.
Mothers were being parted from their sons, and they
From them for many months. There was nothing
To be done, except observe the customary rites:
Baba Devlet, Father State, had intervened. You too
Were drafted, but, on your way to Okinawa,
Had the good luck to contract hepatitis, spending
The rest of your war at a typewriter in Saipan.
Once, in Van, I asked a Kurdish friend
What it was like to serve in the Turkish army,
And he said: 'Oh, it wasn't so bad really.
I was stationed near the Bulgarian border.
There was nothing to do, so I read Turgenev.'
So perhaps these great demonstrations of feeling
Were disproportionate, but that would be
To think in temperate, English terms, and I wasn't
In England was I? The bus veered south into
A land of lunar ventifacts and umbrella pines,
Where the *Mistress of Beasts* once dwelt in
Niches at the foot of geometric façades resembling
Tapestries and carpets. Rainstorms still pursued us.
Horizons turned to a calamitous black,
And the streets of obscure towns steamed
In the sun, and, strange to report, until you were eighteen,
Meteorology had been your favoured vocation.
The war changed that, and you became a poet,
Never thereafter swerving from that perplexed
Calling. This, perhaps, is immaterial. Is it
Likely you would have become a stockbroker?
Perhaps you could have *mixed cement*, but
I sincerely doubt it, though you would certainly
Have described with sympathy the intimate
Feelings of the cement. When, at last, I arrived
In Afyon, another weeping woman with water
In her hands made as if to run after a bus,
But fainted, and was carried to a bench in the shade.
There was sympathy, but it was clear the episode
Was considered unexceptional as earth or water.

Afyon means opium and, at the right season,
Ivory-white and purple poppies delight the eye.
What is more, its full name (which no one uses)
Is Afyon Karahisar, which can be rendered
In English as Opium Black Citadel, and, yes, a tall
Black rock crowned by crenellated ramparts
Looms over an old quarter of painted houses
With projecting sunrooms from which
The women of past times could observe the life
Of the street without themselves being observed,
And listen to the songs of the water-carriers.
It is one of many places in Turkey I would have
Liked to show you, but now never will. I stayed
In a hotel with an absurdly vast atrium,
And, at once, was returned in mind to the lavish
And equally absurd public spaces of private buildings
In Manhattan (which I love to distraction, but,
To my great sadness, am unlikely to ever revisit).
I sat down to write and recalled the gloomy dining-
Room, where, for some months, I sifted through
The deep strata of your unpublished manuscripts.
I'm not sure my labours were of much use to you,
But you knew I was hard up, and this was your way
Of helping. Thank you. I remember
With particular affection a 'translation'
Of Rimbaud into pure, American teenspeak.
I laughed outloud. Thank you again. As I began
To write what turned out to be an enormous letter
To the woman I regretted to have to call your widow,
I thought of the time you had both arrived
In Istanbul, and how much you had enjoyed the place,
Still eager for *Fresh Air* in your seventies,
Although the food seemed to puzzle you (it was all
Too preludial, somehow), and how, at the reading,
It was discovered that the translation of *One Train*
Was incomplete, which perhaps, in retrospect,
Sounds a premonitory false note, and how the boys
On the front desk of the Pera Palas Hotel
Had been so thrilled that a real poet was their guest
That they asked if they could borrow for a night

All the books you'd given me, so they could copy them,
Which they did. That I thought, was immortality
Of some kind, and I plunged deeper into unknown
Places – Akraonia, Eumeneia – returning
Each evening to write another page of the letter,
And read your work as I ate my long, solitary,
But contented suppers. As to the friend, why
Did I need his company when I had you in print?
Later, much later, your magnificent *Collected*
Poems arrived at my Istanbul address,
And I shared them with my students. How
They loved, without reservation, *One Train*,
Our Hearts and *The Problem of Anxiety*, all new
To them. It was as if a wall had been removed:
They got your jokes, and saw something that
Moved under them that had to do with their lives.
One of them wrote: 'I like Kenneth Koch's poetry
Very much. I think he was a very generous man
Who brought poetry to many people, and helped them.
This surprised me completely, because I thought poetry
Was always difficult.' Kenneth, I gave her an A.

Prose for Ebubekir Akbulut

Asiens Atem ist jenseits.

Ingeborg Bachmann,
Grosse Landschaft Bei Wien

1

Made of steel and black, the door to the building
Gets harder to open by the day. It is like a door
Of basalt in the dry hills of the Hauran, still turning
On hinges of basalt (the hardest of volcanic rocks)
After millennia, and the houses trabeate
And still fit to live in, a miracle! Beyond
(In this poem everything, it seems, is beyond something)
In the hallway, an ugly sofa stands on end, tied
With a light blue thread, close to a cabinet
Made of the cheapest wood. (Is it wood at all?
It looks all veneer.) Under the frescoed ceiling
With its *trompe l'oeil* coffers, in musty late-Ottoman
Gloom, they look almost monumental, tombstones
At the very least… I think this must mean
That my upstairs neighbours have moved out.
My feelings are mixed. They came I think (I would guess
From their music) from the ruined Black Sea coast,
Somewhere east of Samsun, from which anyone
With wit escapes. They thundered and crashed
Above me with abandon. I used to shout through the ceiling
Like an ogre or a madman in a fit to the effect of,
'Cut it out willya?' Sometimes they did, but now
They are gone to a district poorer and more remote,
Filled with dust or mud according to the season,
And a scattering of antique American cars, broken
And repaired times beyond number (as if there were
A useful number for time in this place). What
Will happen next is up for grabs. They flooded me (twice),
But once extinguished a fire in my wastebasket,
While I, heedless, was out shopping for salad greens.

Water I had learned to consider, in part because of
Their charitable ministrations, but fire turned a new page
Of scrambled letters, most likely in cuneiform or
The Phrygian alphabet. I couldn't get my head around it.
If I had fallen asleep would I have died like Ingeborg Bachmann –
Alone, alone, after strong liquor, a cigarette falling from my hand?

2

These are powerful enigmas occluded from sense
Like the lump in the floor at the foot of the stairs
That looks as if it 'heaved a sigh', and then froze,
The largely submerged iceberg of this architecture –
Cherishable, sullied, nostalgic and decayed. O,
So many adjectives! We can surely do without these,
But we cannot. What does it mean to *describe*?
Aside from the fact that it is like pasting wet leaves
To a column, we can only guess, as we do with such certainty
About the reasons for the Bronze Age collapse,
Which, in fact, is wholly inexplicable, as so far determined:
We only know that large numbers of people suddenly
Began to move around at great speed over vast distances,
Trashing everything in their path: cities, languages,
Artworks, trade routes, economies and literatures,
As, sadly, people are wont to do in the streets of our cities,
However white and grey and blue and orderly they appear.
Then there is what we call technology to confuse
And charm us, albeit leavened or laden
With generous doses of refined, professional boredom
(Are these ideas? Is this A Poem of Ideas? O help!
Words come to my aid. *There* that's better). It is
All irreducible, fissiparous. Where, in Istanbul,
For example, is the oxness of an ox, an ox that towed
Veiled women along the paths of Europe and Asia,
In curtained carts, to springs, fountains, woods and lawns,
Where they could rest and disclose themselves to each other?
Those idylls are blasted and the women, whom
Histories recount, were of exceptional beauty, are shut
In their tombs, which are domed, octagonal,

Harmoniously proportioned like a Platonic Ideal.
It is at once beyond and within the limits of our
Intellective grasp, like sheets of water flowing on Mars,
Or not flowing, as the case may be...

3

Five flights up, on a windowsill, someone
Has thoughtfully placed a white, flowering plant,
Which grows from a bulbous brown pot. I am grateful
For its presence, but will I ever learn its name?
Botany, I have neglected you, but how numinous
Are your names, written in a language long dead
To the millions who, in spirit, we know as well as
Our nail parings: they are with us now and oppressed
As if an immense, baroque cloud like an opera
Of malicious intent hung over them, reducing
Everything to ash or some other worthless compound,
Obscuring the names of things and places that I love
To distraction, names of rivers and mountains, names
Of cities with mosaics that are to be drowned,
And lead us by way of inhabited vine-scrolls,
And the bearded visages of river gods (Euphrates,
Orontes) to an altered region of poplar groves and lakes,
Where we might have lived idly, and *sans souci*...
Names, how can you ever be numbered or pronounced –

Dvin, Ebla, Uruk, Mkhseta, Ctesiphon, Araxa?

I will go to these places one day, as I will go to Ur,
And come back full of a busy wisdom, and spooked.
They are not to be known, but can be perceived
Remotely, like the first flower you remember.
Was it white or yellow? Blue as in woad or
A periwinkle? Did that woman standing outside
The church of a vulgar novel (a wedding scene,
A gunshot) wear a wide hat made of a very
Light material? It was summer. My father, dark
(Sad) horse, knew her, though not biblically, since
That was more a muffled business of erections in parks,

And public urinals. Let that pass. It is out of time,
And imagining. He is dead now, and my resentments
Have withered like an ancient hand. Beyond that
Nothing is certain, except that we love all that it gives us
(I mean nothing) like a rose in a Mallarmé sonnet
Of, I suppose, Petrarchan form. Absence is a French word,
And there is more to it: tarnished or clear, the mirror
Cannot reflect the sky or the river, place it as you may.

4

Old and creaking, the apartment's double
Wooden doors rattle in the wind. Open them
A crack and the past crowds in like forest or snow,
We don't know how to escape this, and perhaps
There is no need to: it is like this and we require
No further divagations from the theme.
The windows give voice in a baffling polyphony
Of knocks and thuds, in sore need of a strict baton
(Stroke upon stroke). The scorched floor is by now
Mere aggravation. Damage is limited. It's not as if
I'm obligated to live in the rubble of a war, except
In the sense that we all do on a permanent basis
Like the immovable pedestal of a looted statue,
Representing, in allegory, some too-familiar concept,
Extinguished Hope, perhaps, or *Ironic Acceptance*.
This, in the end, is a poem of that climate
We are gifted. Gifts come to us unlooked for.
Pure clouds rise in towering accumulations,
And the rug, cured of the filth of the fire, has been
Returned, which is more than could be hoped for
Like spring in January. For now, all that matters
Are the exactingly formalised sprigs in the design.
If they had burned, how many years of mute love
And unsung toil would have been lost. Something
Is present (a shadow) that escapes me like a wish
Or a sigh. The many reds glow, but not with the colours
Of fire or blood, while, above the ceiling's stucco medallion,
Silence settles into absence like the dead waters of a lake.

The Antiochiad

The boys at the next table were getting emotional.
One stood up and made as if to leave, but was
Persuaded to stay. Another wept copiously.
The handsomest youth was the one who remained calm,
And reasoned with the rest. But what could have inspired
Such a collective fit of passion? Intrigued,
I introduced myself. At once, they insisted
That I join them, and summoned the musicians.
Then the questions began. Where was I from?
What was I doing in Ankara? Where did I live?
Where was I going? How far, how long, and why?
I was not always able to answer, but this was ritual,
Not interrogation, and intended to set a lone stranger
At his ease. To them I was a gift. The imperative
Of welcome overruled their sadness, and they laughed,
Forgetting the vicissitudes of love and work.
In the morning Arda came to the hotel,
And we drove south, along with Nevra and Inal.
Only Pelin did not come with us, which saddened me a little.
The road ran straight across the emptiness of the plateau
Beside a salt lake like an inland sea. (Once,
Years past, I saw a full moon rise over it.)
Nevra said, in a tone that brooked no argument:
'John, your legs are so long you must sit in the front.'
I was embarrassed, but though all three of them
Were pressed together in the back, no one complained
Or grew fractious. Instead, they engaged in quiet,
Good-humoured conversation until we stopped
To eat on the outskirts of Aksaray, beneath which lies
A city founded by Archelaus, last king of Cappadocia.
Barely a stone of it remains visible amid orchards,
And the dispersed waters of the Melendiz. Snowclad,
(It was December) Mount Hasan rose to the south.
This was a land of miracles and mirages,
Where lakes and inverted pine-forests appeared
And dissolved in seconds. We descended, by degrees,
To the Cilician Gates, great, inscribed defile,

And conduit of armies. The air grew suddenly warmer.
The Taurus rose on either side, and shadows of figures
Came to mind. I thought of Nikephoros Phokas –
Ugly, obstinate, honourable – leading his troops
Against double-walled Tarsus, confident of victory,
Entirely unaware of the terrible fate that awaited him –
His dismembered corpse thrown from a balcony,
Bleeding into banks of snow. Beyond the Gates,
The land opened like a fan. There was no time
To stop at Tarsus, which I regretted, remembering
A feast of grilled trout and pickled herbs
Beside the waterfalls. Also, we passed by Adana,
And Anazarbus, across the broad Cilician Plain.
There were cotton fields, factories emitting
Sulphureous smoke, and castles of the Armenians.
Above Alexandretta we climbed towards
The Syrian Gates; I was reminded of the road
From Beirut to the Bekaa, but the walls of Belen
Were unmarked by shells or mortars, and a belfry
Rose from a high cluster of houses. The summit
Passed, the road swept down in a vast curve,
Like an extravagant gesture of welcome, towards
The Plain of Amuq, where once there had been
A shallow lake in which the Seleucid elephants,
So beloved of the people of Antioch, had waded at leisure.
(But that was before Magnesia and Pydna.)
Here began the road to Bactria and Sogdiana,
To Arachosia, the theatre of Our Lady Moon,
Euripides on the Oxus, Buddha as Apollo...

The outskirts of the city were uninviting
(Auto-repair, scrap-metal, ruinous workshops)
And the Orontes was so rigidly embanked
That it resembled a drainage ditch crossed by
Ugly, skeletal bridges. Was this what was called,
In Arabic, The Rebellious One? Snow had fallen
On Mount Silpios. In the courtyard of a mosque
There were orange trees, heavy with fruit,
And tall cypresses. The vaults of the prayer hall
Were carried on massive, antique, granite columns.

I walked along twisting lanes so narrow,
The eaves of houses almost met above my head. Here,
Life was lived behind tall, ornamented doors,
In courtyards, and on terraces planted with fruit trees,
Entirely hidden from view, labyrinth and cloister,
From which there was no need to escape. In the morning,
Warm rain came down in torrents. My shoes leaked,
And I sought refuge in the Mosaic Museum, where
Orpheus plied his lyre, attended by a rapt chorus
Of animals and stones, and an over-eager Psyche,
Like a pantomime fairy, ran towards her
Drowsy avatar, and a serving-maid presented
Her mistress with a tray of jewellery and cosmetics,
While, close by, the Happy Hunchback flaunted
His enormous member. Here, surely, were the people
Who had derided priggish, philosophical Julian
(At least, if Cavafy's account can be believed).
At Daphne, the grove of the nymph was violated.
The waiters were surly, the temple gone, and the oracle dumb.
It was hard to believe that so much had vanished –
The hecatombs of oxen, the villas with peristyles...
What we know does not assist the eye:
The street of columns, the oval plaza, Trajan's column,
Entombed under centuries of accumulated silt.
We cannot go there, so we observe, and wonder as
Best we can amid *the little that remains*, which is
Somehow always enough for us, and perhaps too much:
Those murderous or murdered monarchs seem to
Gibber and grimace from the brittle pages of the books,
Leaving no memento save a sister's severed hand,
Or a cup of poisoned wine offered by a mother to her son,
Which he, instead, forced her to drink. And yet you say,
Extenuating, there was art and learning. Yes,
And the lucubrations of philosophers, who could not
Tell the heart from the brain, who aspired only
To *stasis*, cessation of pain, *ataraxia*, despising
All things merely banausic, even the making
Of a figured bowl, or the operation of a waterwheel.
On Silpios' summit, the car skidded in snow,
And a crowd of dogs burst from an isolated house.

The day was overcast, but, as we were about to leave,
A single shaft of light illumined the distant sea,
And Seleucia, where once I was 'arrested',
On my way to the acropolis, by cheerful militiamen
Who fed me pastries, and sweet, dark tea.
This seemed to me simple goodness. I had entered
A forbidden zone, but, because of my ignorance,
They forgave me, and introduced me to their families.
The small room looked out towards the snows
Of Mount Cassius and the harbour from which
Heraclius departed, crying bitterly: 'Farewell,
A long farewell to Syria.' It was to protect this harbour
From the fate of Ephesus that the Emperors Titus
And Vespasian ordered a tunnel to be driven
Through a mountain, diverting flood waters. It began
As a simple cutting, curving up from the shore.
Water ran in a channel. The walls grew higher,
Sloping inwards until they closed above us.
The local boys were afraid to go further. Light
From airshafts, falling through veils of water,
Bathed the stone in tones of purple and umber.
I emerged, at length, into a bright glade to which
There seemed no other means of access, and saw,
A thousand feed above, the scattered houses
Of a village, under a white haze of woodsmoke.

That evening, Nevra returned late
From an official reception and summoned me
To the lobby: 'John, you must have a raki.
It was so *boring*. These politicians are stupid.
Tomorrow, I want to see something. Anything…'
So we went to the cave-church of Saint Peter.
Curative waters oozed from the walls, and
From a rock-face a figure of Charon kept
Brooding watch over the foundations of a city gate,
But this was not what drew my attention.
Close by, a ravine led deep into Silpios
My eyes itched with the memory of a map
(Schematic, misleading), and an obscure phrase
Came to my mind: *the torrent called Onopnikles.*

Without knowing, I knew where the path led,
And at once, a small, ragged boy ran up,
Asking: 'Do you want to see the castle?'
Of course I did. He pointed out his home,
Which was a shed clinging to a rock, albeit
Equipped with certain vents for the release
Of 'noxious emissions'. So the boy grew, stunted,
But trained in the exquisite manner of his grandparents.
We walked in amicable silence. I forgot my friends,
Thinking only of what might lie ahead.
We passed between two, flanking towers. Was this
The castle? No, it was much bigger, and further off.
The ravine narrowed. We scrambled over boulders
Draped with ribbons of trash, and the boy shouted *kale*,
And there it was, *The Iron Gate* of which I had read
So often in accounts of the many sieges of Antioch –
High wall of perfect, Justinianic ashlar,
Pierced by an arch. I had not known it still existed
But how was I to reward the child who had
Shown me this wonder? Too much might corrupt,
Too little insult. I chose what seemed to me
A modest sum, but our perceptions were different.
He looked into his hand as if the sun shone out of it,
And ran off at the speed with the bill crushed in a fist
Held high. At the hotel, Nevra told me
That when she had returned without me,
The manager became very agitated.
Perhaps something had happened to me.
Perhaps I had *fallen off the mountain*.
To which Nevra replied: 'No, it is John.
He has found something.' In the evening,
A family invited us to their home. We admired
The salon, the terrace, the beautiful kitchen,
But most of all, we admired the flourishing
Bergamot tree, hung with fruits the size of footballs,
From the rind of which a fragrant oil can be
Extracted. I had thought the name derived from
Bergamo or Bergama. Not so. The root is Turkish –
Beğ-armut, meaning Lord of Pears, which it
Categorically is not, being a citrus fruit

Of Chinese origin that made its slow way
Westwards in the years that followed Alexander.
In the morning, the driver could not be found.
Inal stamped up and down, calling him a 'donkey',
And doubtless some worse things I didn't understand,
But in the end, we were able to leave, returning
Through the Double Gates to our lives within
Sight and hearing of the strait that divided us.
Months later I suddenly recalled that strange
Passage through the mountain, the hidden glade,
When I chanced upon translations of Orphic fragments
That had been inscribed on gold-leaf in a Cretan tomb:

'On the left-hand of the House of Hades
You will find a wellspring, and beside it
A white cypress. Do not approach, but walk
A little further, and you will find another
With cool water flowing forth from the Lake
Of Memory. Here stand the Guardians,
Whom you must address in this fashion. Say
To them: *I am a child of earth, but my destiny
Is of Heaven. This you know well. I am parched
With thirst and I perish. Give me quickly
Of the cool waters that spill from the Lake of Memory.*
Be assured that they will answer your plea,
And permit you to drink your fill. Thereafter,
You will dwell in the company of heroes,
Having escaped forever from the cycle of sorrows.'